On The Face Of It

C J Lewis

Illustrations by Mark Anthony Carroll

Edited by Roy McFarlane

Financial Assistance given by Sunrise Bakery

An environmentally friendly book printed and bound in England
by www.printondemand-worldwide.com

Mixed Sources
Product group from well-managed forests, and other controlled sources
www.fsc.org Cert no. TT-COC-002641
© 1996 Forest Stewardship Council

PEFC Certified
This product is from sustainably managed forests and controlled sources
www.pefc.org
PEFC/16-33-415

This book is made entirely of chain-of-custody materials

FastPrint Publishing
www.fast-print.net/store.php

ON THE FACE OF IT

A catalogue record for this book is available from the British Library

ISBN 978-178456-100-0

First published 2014 by
FASTPRINT PUBLISHING
Peterborough, England.

Acknowledgments

I am truly grateful to my editor Roy McFarlane who took time and great care to appraise the collection by advising me and making valid suggestions.

My sincere thanks to fellow poet Sue Brown who has been instrumental and inspirational in reviewing my manuscript and giving invaluable comments.

Many, many thanks and love to my daughter Michelle. It would not have been possible for this anthology to materialise without her help and many hours of typing on the computer producing several drafts before this final manuscript.

Thanks to my son Mark for his creativity in producing the illustrations for the collection.

Thanks to my son Winston for transporting me to various venues for performances which has helped to develop my poetry over the last decade.

Appreciation and reflection of my late sister Ruby for being a good role model in my early developing years. The poem I have dedicated to her titled *'Good Memories'* sums up my feelings for her.

The following poem is in dedication of my beloved late sister Ruby

Good Memories

My thoughts, my feelings,
my memories of my sister so dear.
She was always full of praise and cheer,
not showing any fear.
Not biased but fair
with dignity and flair.

Ruby was her name,
to me and many others she was a dame
who was not seeking fortune or fame.
With no children of her own
substitute mother she became
for others and me she treated the same,
honesty and love was her game.

Her love had no boundaries,
family, friends and foe,
heaven knows,
their needs and problems she would address,
no charges would be made
no matter how great the cost.

Her infectious laughter
was part of her character.
Her kindness and generosity overwhelming,
her beautiful voice astounding.
Her name reflects her value.

Ruby a priceless jewel
as everyone's needs she would fulfil.
My sister Ruby was like an earthly angel,
an example to the human race.
Her absence are trials and grief
we must face.

The legacy of love,
she has left behind,
none better you could find.
Like a fountain flowing in all directions
far and wide.
I can still remember her with great pride,
she had nothing to hide.

Young and old,
here and there,
wherever they abide
still speaks her name with fondest memories
roaring like the tide.

Her name,
Mother Ruby,
our Ruby and precious stone,
my sister Ruby,
with such memories of you I will never be alone.

Introduction

On The Face Of Its' collection delves deeply within the tapestry of life taking the readers seamlessly through myriad forms of life experiences, reality, fantasy and expectations.

The collection has transformed everyday challenges and mundane situations into laughter, love and reflections with a focus on life's forever changing faces where fantasy and reality mingles effortlessly within the art of everyday living.

Seasoned verses with a flair of exuberance laced with humour and thought provoking metaphors, it provides a place where lyrical memories lingers whilst thoughts and actions of today and tomorrow grows from mustard seeds to big acorns.

On reflection, some readers may identify with situations highlighted in the poems whether it be political correctness or the raw facts of life which affects mind body and soul.

Likewise the collection may introduce the reader to an experience they may not have had before.

To add some Caribbean flavour, a few of the poems are written in Jamaican Patois (pronounced Patwa).

A glossary is provided as an interpretation aid if required.

Contents

On The Face Of It

*'All the world's a stage
and one man in his time
plays many parts.'

On the face of it
game changers we are.
Dark clouds or shining stars?
Realities or dreams?
Facts or fiction?
Everyone has many roles to play,
that is the nature of the game.

On the face of it
the daily situations of
sadness or happiness,
excitement or mundaneness
is the tapestry of life,
the art of everyday living.

On the face of it
young or old,
rich or poor,
black or white,
yellow or brown,
strands of life interwoven
or broken
dictates our destiny
whatever the age
on this ever changing world stage.

(*Quote from As You Like It, Act 2, Sc. 7 written by William Shakespeare.)

The Edge

On the edge of life she rode
daring to live her dreams.
Dreams filled with danger
and excitement,
each experience brings tears,
joy or fulfilment
knowing that every living fibre
of her being screams
Life!
Life!

On the edge of power she clambered
embracing challenges and success
along the way.
On the art of success she focussed each day.

On the edge of darkness and despair
she found hope.
Positive thoughts, words and actions
Engraved in her philosophy.
Every defeat, every triumph is viewed
like a kaleidoscope,
living on life's edge provides a wide scope.

On the edge of life she rode,
on the edge of power she clambered.
On the edge of darkness and despair
she found hope.

What a Difference a Day Makes

Yesterday my love you were my precious dove
sent to me by wishing stars from above.
The two of us so much in love,
no anger, no wrath in our hearts,
such great joy did light our path.

Our favourite meeting place
your beauty did grace
as we embraced,
completely lost in time and space.

Oblivious of others around us
we listened to the wonderful
sounds of birds singing
and the ripples of the water,
each ripple
made our hearts quiver.

In the glade
where we first laid,
all beautiful and tranquil.
We prayed all our dreams would be fulfilled,
not that you would be killed.

The small trees, brambles and sticks
listened as we whispered words
of love it was sheer bliss.
Many a picnic we had,
there was no time to be sad
as I pretended to be jack the lad.
Wild flowers decorated our bed and table of grass.
Alas such wonderful moments have passed.

The berries we picked and ate, wild and exotic
even hypnotic
as we kissed with reddened lips.
Only tenderness was embedded in your fingertips.

The sun, the blue skies and even clouds were not allowed to
intrude
upon our interlude.

The tree we carved with our names so dear
is now lying in despair,
freshly chopped and arranged to accommodate your head.

Placed between two halves,
your arms outstretched as if this is your cross
and your hour has passed.

Wild flowers adorned your lovely frame.
I can still hear you
calling my name.
To love and be loved was our game.

How dare they separate thee from me!
The large tree that bore witness to our love
and indulgence now holds the secret
of this fatal day.

There are no answers for me
even as I kneel and pray.
Today my love,
my joy has turned to sorrow,
there can be no tomorrow.

After thee I shall follow,
it is not goodbye my love
but soon we shall meet
at lovers retreat
my precious dove.

(Inspired by the painting 'Now the Leaves are Falling Fast' by Anya Gallaccio, from the 2004 'Forest' exhibition at the Wolverhampton Art Gallery).

Revenge

My man Stan, he was my greatest fan
I would say up to the other day.

Upon him all my love I had bestowed,
no holds barred at any time he could
mark my card.

So to hear our friend say
that with this wench he did stay
for a whole night and a day,
for me sheer dismay.

The first thought that entered my head
was to knock him dead
until my friend said
a *'Bobbitt' would be
more deserving and the wench
could have it as a serving,
for a starter, main course
or dessert as this was sure to hurt.

Stan my ex man now lacks the urge
and desire to flirt
with a skirt or a shirt.

(*John Wayne Bobbitt's ex-wife Lorena cut off almost half his penis after alleged extra marital affairs and alleged emotional and physical abuse.)

Cover me with your love

Like a warm blanket
on a cold winter's night
I need you to hold me tight.
I need you to say
everything is alright.

As our bodies entwined
such closeness,
my skin,
your skin,
hear and feel
the love which flows within.

Cover me with your love
like the fresh fallen snow
on a winter's morn.
Like a baby held close
in its' mother's arms
the moment it's born.
My skin,
your skin,
feel the love
which flows within,
the love which flows within.

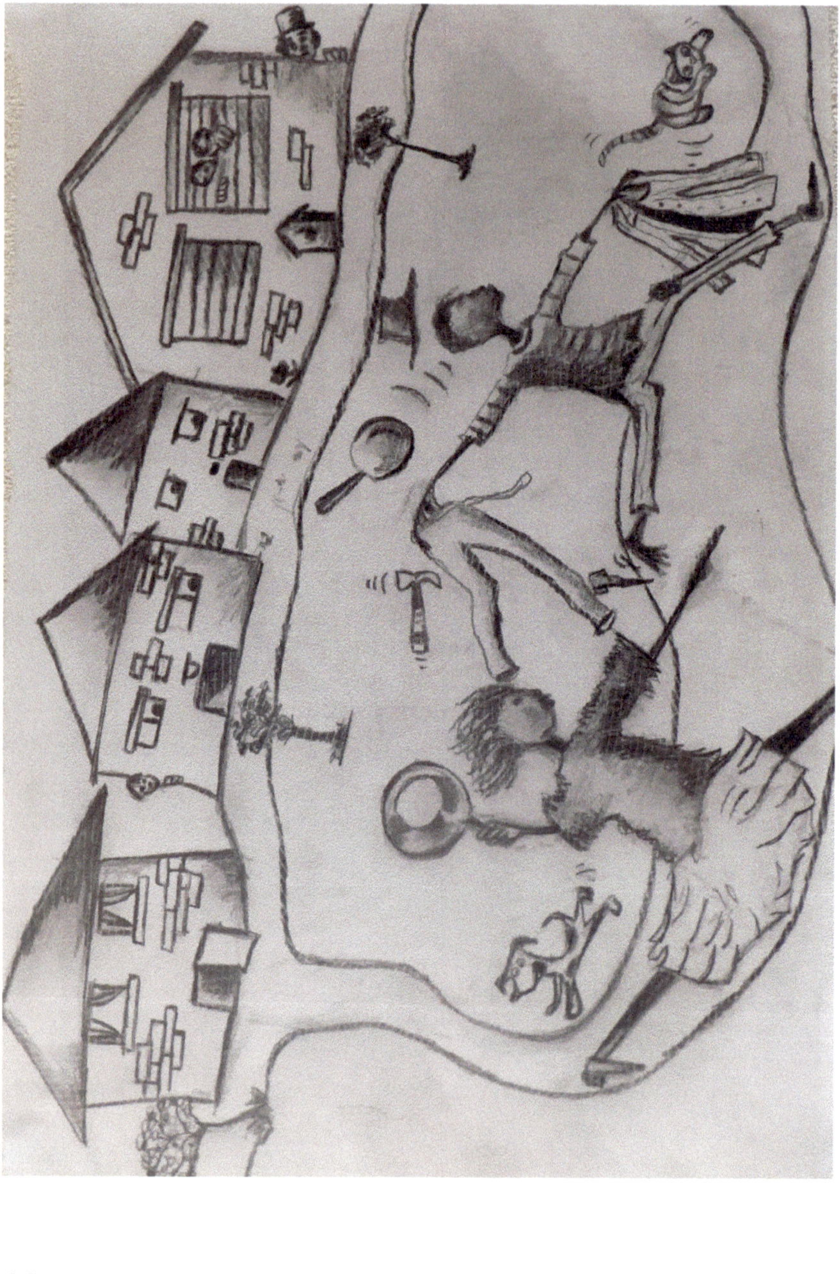

Run for Cover

Every so often
she went off on one.
Everything would fly
including pots and pans,
not forgetting her
bruised and battered man.

For cover he ran,
shirt and pants in hand,
cat and dog in pursuit,
neighbours' curtains
twitching, guessing who
would end up in a heap
or who would be dead meat!

Words So Often Heard

They say the best things in life are free
and it applies to you and me.
You say free for who?
I say maybe for you but not for me.
Words so often heard.

You asked what is best?
They flounder
for words as if it was a tricky test.
Love and best.
Words so often heard.

They say love is blind,
I asked what is love?
you say the path is hard to find.
They say it's a thing that
makes you feel good or bad inside
depending on the tide.
Words so often heard.

I say love can make you kind or unkind
to your fellow mankind.
They say it makes the world
go round.
You say it depends on where you are bound.
Love and world.
Words so often heard.

I asked which world?
First, second or third?
secular, spiritualist?
or any others on the list
Words so often heard.

They say, you say, I say.
You get older and wiser, you say, but look on the
price you had to pay...............***Words so often heard.***

Missing Links

There are several missing links
from my broken chain.
I need to ascertain
from which tribe I came.
What is my real name?
and who directly is to blame?

The transportation of my ancestors
from Africa to the Caribbean
begs many a question.
Slavery, abolition,
emancipation, colonisation,
words used in a myriad of ways,
what are their connotations?

Can those missing links
be found written in ink?
A culture lost by many a generation
has left me in sheer isolation.

I am like a tree without roots,
branches without leaves,
a busted cultural chain.
I am still searching, searching
for those missing links.

Where and Who is the Daddy?

As a boy growing up into this harsh world,
only negative things about my father I was told.
My mother would say
every single day
"Your father was no good
only for bad things he stood,
a ruffian and a hooligan."

My sister, myself and younger brother
who gave a lot of bother
would move from place to place,
how could we have guessed
that it was to ensure that
our whereabouts our father could not trace
as in each place we started anew
for all to view.
My mother pushing the pram,
my sister and I close by.

You could guarantee that
by some nosey neighbours
the same questions would be asked
where is the father?
and
who is the father?
The answer we knew so well
as my mother to them would tell
"Their father is dead,
you can find him in hell!"
That was the story she had to tell.

Those words over and over I did dread,
you can imagine how I felt.
At the age of twenty
into my life the ruffian hooligan
dead father made an entry.

On face book,
as a last resort
he looked.

As his story unfolded
the anger inside me
towards my mother exploded.
This kind gentle man
not a ruffian or a hooligan,
hugged me like a father should.
All those lost years
we were both in tears.

No longer consumed with fears
of the unknown
as such fatherly love
I'm now being shown,
a love which is so right and strong
and soon it won't be long
before my son arrives.
He will not be deprived
of that fatherly bond and love
for which I had craved and longed.

Cloning

When I was young,
the lashing of my mother's tongue
was no fun.
Even now in bed
I can recall what was said.

"Janiceeeee!"
"Yes mama."
"Why have you not made the bed
the way I said?"
"But mama,"
"don't you but me!"
"Janiceeee! why are you washing and sweeping today?
You done know say you must do them on a Friday?

Sundays is to praise the Lord
not to wash or Sweep the yard.
Janiceeee!"
"Yes mama."
Why are you asking me for rice and peas,
chicken and other delicacies
in the middle of the week?"
my mother squeak.
"Girl is it attention that you seek?"
"But mama!"
"Gal don't even bother to speak."

"Janiceeee! hurry up and wash your cup,
we are going to the market
fe go try we luck,
we must not be late.
At any rate
it is the early bird that catches the worm."
"What worm mama?"
"Child don't ask no question,
Saturday is the day we go to the market,
me grandmother, me mother and now me,
without tradition you don't have any culture."

That was the day I decided that this traditional ritual
mumbo jumbo stopped with me.
Passed on to my children?
Never!
But why was I not told that being a mother
was a job like no other
and that my mother
was now so much like my grandmother.

The other day
my sister came to stay.
A family occasion it was,
she looked at me confused
and bemused
as my daughter's request for rice and peas on a Tuesday was refused.
I barked ***"Jessica it is Uncle John's funeral today."***
"Yes mom" she replied.
"So why are you wearing that red dress?
Are you trying to cause me stress?

We always wear black to funerals,
have some respect."
My sister shook her head
and cut me dead,
then muttered **"cloning."**
Oh God, I have turned into my mother!
This made me shudder.
Genetics or traditions my mould is well set,
my cloning is complete.
The lashing of my tongue now beats in Jessica's ears like a drum.

Holier Than Thou

I am a Christian,
and not a sinner like you.
I know the bible
through and through.
I am special that is my view,
I am not a sinner like you.

Genesis to Revelations
is my portion.
You have no notion about
dedication.
I am not into all those worldly
celebration,
no matter what the occasion.
You see I am a Christian
and not a sinner like you.

Every Sunday I go to church,
some people say I leave my family
in the lurch so my conscience
I must search.
See I am a Christian
and not a sinner like you.

I am one of the chosen few,
in heaven I shall be.
Brimstone and fire will be heaped
upon you.
See I am a Christian
and not a sinner like you.

The Ten Commandments you must follow,
a copy from me you can borrow.
To church you must go
to be a Christian like me
and not a sinner like you.

Sky Fall

As you fall from the sky
in dust and flakes
so light,
so white,
a beautiful sight
on many a moonlit night.

On a sunny winter's day
your presence lay
covering the trees
and their branches,
you are so picturesque.

The scenery you enhance,
a sheer winter wonderland.
So light,
so white,
a beautiful sight.

Moonlight

The moon is shining bright,
Trees glistened from its' bathing light
What great delight!
Oh beautiful moonlight
You are a magnificent sight,
Enhancing everything in your path.
You are at the heart of many lovers dreams
As they stride hand in hand in lovers land,
Your beams penetrating deep in their inner beings.

Your shining light bright or dim
Breaking through clouds thick or thin.
In starry skies universally you shine
On the grass wet with dew,
On the trees and across the lakes,
There is no mistake that like the wind blows
Where it pleases your light beams with tranquillity,
Oozes with personality and ability.

The continuous changing of your size and shape
Cause many a debate.
Sometimes you are full bodied,
At other times you are half with a different shape.
Entwined with the sun expressing your magical skills,
An eclipse is the result when you kiss.

Oh beautiful one your creation is everything magical
Your presence enchanting for many precious moments
Factual or mythical.
From whence you came and where you go
Will always be part of nature's show.

Keys to My Heart

Right from the very start,
you dearly held the keys to my heart,
from you I cannot bear to be apart.

It may seem absurd that you and I should have met
and connect,
those precious keys to you I entrusted.
Oh my dearest
do not allow me to forget
the sweetness of our love.

And as time passes by
we will reflect on those precious memories
we shared knowing that
the keys to my heart is still kept in a safe place.
That place my love is you.

Changing Faces

I am who I am.
I am whom I wanted to be.
I am me.
My ever changing faces
for all to see.
My heart and brain dictates
the contours of my face,
things and situations
also joins in the race.

Genetics generates the colour
to the skin on my face
as it did to my kit and kin,
black, white, yellow or brown
brings a smile or a frown.

As my inner feelings
displays outer expression
and changes,
those viewing me may be confused
as to my mood and persona.
I am who I am.
I am whom I wanted to be.
I am me.
My ever changing faces
for all to see.

Stillness

So still yet so perfectly formed,
alive or dead,
no leaves to shed,
still there is so much to be said.

Sculptured and captured
in full glories,
tells numerous stories.
Ageless, changeless,
speechless, stillness,
multi-facets,
greatest of assets.

You are looking at me
when there are others to see.
Frozen in time,
am I cold?
am I old?
Unsure,
yet my beauty as you see
draws you to me.

Come closer,
what blemishes can you see?
If any
do not replenish me.
Am I old or young?
I can be any age at this stage.
Undated and preserve,
your judgment I reserve.

What your eyes are seeing,
is it the same as what your mind is saying?
Where and what are your thoughts now?

Stillness.

(Inspired by the sculpture 'Morning fog in the mountains' by Mariele Neudecker exhibited at the 2004 'Forest' exhibition at Wolverhampton Art Gallery)

Discovery

Where am I?
Lost in the denseness and darkness of life
so it seems,
reality or dreams?
Overshadowed by fears of the unknown.
Helplessly trapped I sat on my own
seeking confirmation and clarity,
this was no dream it was reality.

My mind like a glade waiting to be filled
with ideas that will be transformed
into empowerment
or disappointment,
what is it to be?
I cannot wait any longer to see,
this is about me.

A flickering of light within me stirred.
Ideas emerged as the adrenaline surged.
Emotional waves of my inner being
gradually becoming stronger.
Insufficient at first to transform my outer expression of
contemplation.

The myriad of choices I could make at this junction of life
filled the empty spaces in my mind.
Rays of light suddenly beamed into the darkest
hour of my life.
A clear and sunny path is now in sight,
in my mind I have found the right path.

For my sake, this journey I have to take.
Leaving the past is no easy task.
I am now wearing my new mask.

Embracing the future,
my ideas I must nurture.

At this juncture excitement is tinged
with fears and trepidation.
I suddenly stopped in my tracks
from a brief moment of panic attacks.

Can I live up to others and my own expectations?
But this is no time for procrastination.
Instant dismissal of these thoughts,
my newly found strengths must not be fraught.
As my body and mind travels through the change curve,
I strengthened my nerve,
a purpose well served.

Metaphorically there is a bright light
beyond the forest of my life.
A new horizon now in sight.
I have discovered me.
My inner fears,
my strength,
my resilience
I now embrace.
Just wait and see the new me.

(Author's interpretation of photographs taken by Sally Waterman entitled Forest Fears: Vol II 'Babe in the Wood'. Exhibited in the 2004 'Forest' exhibition at Wolverhampton Art Gallery)

Searching for Love

Love where are you?
I have searched everywhere,

high

&

low

here and.................there

yet I could not find you.
I called you aloud,
I called you in silence,
still you could not be found.
Without you time is passing slowly
and yet quite quickly.

As I search for you,
in my anticipation
my persona at times
becomes quite prickly,
and at times frustration
creeps up in my conversation.
Love I need to find you now!
I want to find you now!
I have to find you now!

When do I call off the search?
In my youth?
In my prime?
In my twilight years?
How will I know if you have
left me in the lurch?

I heard you were in the pub,
I went to find you
hoping together we could
have some grub
but you were not there.

I went to the party to find you,
there was plenty of laughter,
music and dance,
so many seemed to be in a trance,
but love you were not there.

I heard you was in the street,
but we did not meet.
I am now off to a retreat,
this could also spell defeat
but alas we did meet!

My search is over,
as I meditated I found me!
Love you have been here all the time,
beating in my heart,
my four leaf clover,
over and over
staring me in the face
as the love for myself I now embrace.

My love now that I have found you
I will not lose you,
no longer from me can you hide,
inner contentment will be my guide.
My self-confidence, my pride, my joy,
your warmth I will always deploy.

Love you are all around,
you are everywhere,
you are truly in the air.
I am no longer searching, searching,
love you are me, me, me.

My BLBD

From the moment I saw you
I wanted you to be mine.
I had been searching for you
for such a long time.
You are so desirable,
over hot coals and burning flames
I would climb just to ensure
you are mine.
With you I want to dine.

Love at first sight,
this phrase in my case
is so so right.
You are so beautiful I thought
as tears of joy I desperately fought.
You are most wonderful to touch
so pleasing to the eye,
oh I love you so so much,
for you I am willing to die.

You are soft dark and velvety.
Whenever we connect
like glue you cling to my skin
sheer confidence and pleasure kicks in.
Everyone that sees us together
says that we are made for each other,
so compatible, yes inseparable!

My dearest, please
please forgive me
if you felt abused
because so many times
you have been used
but you are my **BLBD**,
my beautiful little black dress.

Broken

Broken, broken.
How could this be?
A bed that was filled with
ecstasy and joy,
screaming with pleasure
at our leisure,
now lonely, cold, uninviting
filled with heartaches and pain.
Was all that love in vain?
Sound of sobs filled the air,
face streaming with tears
unable to control or stem the volume
or the time it flows,
morning, noon or night.

My heart aches,
the pain cuts through
like a knife.
Not so long ago
I felt as though I was in heaven,
my world nearly perfect.
That was the effect
you had on me
my friend,
my lover,
my soul mate.
Today my desire
is for you
to return into my arms,
hold me,
kiss me,
embrace me
and love me
like you used to.

This emptiness and void
cannot and will not
be filled by anyone else
but you my precious love.

Life's Road

Life is like a road leading to everywhere
and sometimes nowhere.
Some paths you take others you forsake.
The journey will have a beginning and an end,
if only we knew what it was to be,
that would be the key.

A lot will depend on what hand mother nature has dealt.
Will it be good family and friends, enemies and foes,
who knows?
Poverty or wealth?
Sickness or health?
Bed of roses or of thorns?
Castle or hovel?
Sadness or happiness?
Life's road is not a joke
but a personal code,
natures destiny mode.

Many milestones and landmarks
along the way.
Conception, a foetus, birth, a baby boy or girl,
a toddler, a young child, a teenager,
an adult, maturity.
This cycle is life's road.

Hopes and dreams,
tears and laughter.
Happiness and disaster,
loyalty and betrayal.
Life's road all sign posted
to its' various turns and paths.
The learning process defeat or success.

The chapters of life with its blue print.
Everyone has to do their stint.
To be born and to die,
a fair road for all is the cry

but the journey may not be so fair,
it will depend on the path
we choose to take or not to take
and sometimes life simply dictates
the paths we tread,
it must be said
this will cement
the lives we've led.

Like all roads and journeys
there is a start and a finish,
a beginning and an end.
Life's road too must end regardless
of what hand mother nature has lend.

Feelings

Emotions emotions emotions,
why and for what do I feel like this?
So many things on my list.
How can I separate my heart from my head?
Mission impossible,
the counsellor said.

Emotions emotions emotions.
Head spinning,
voice singing,
heart in a turmoil,
face has a choice
to smile or not to smile.

Emotions emotions emotions.
The face baring itself to the outside world
and the inner me can be quite different
but this is very hard for you to see.
A chaotic world relates to my thoughts,
is it the whole sum?
Yes at times I do feel numb,
some may even say
I am dumb.

Emotions emotions emotions,
frustration or elation?
The feelings remain
the same.
Manifestation of stress,
even when I am at rest
my mind and body is put to the test.

Emotions emotions emotions,
why and for what do I feel like this?
The cycle has repeated itself
over and over again.
Yet there are still
so many things on my list.
Emotions emotions emotions.

Statement

Clothes maketh a woman I am told,
whether she be young or old.

What kind of woman? I asked.
The answer came flooding back,
(middle class)
in fact whatever her class
she needs to cover her arse.

Society dictates how a woman
should dress to impress.
Scantily clad
will be
sexy for some lad.

Tall and elegant,
appealing to some gent.
Short and skimpy,
medium or long,
she is making a statement.

Look at me,
I love me,
I hate me,
come and get me,
I am out to get you,
piss off!
Crimplene or lace,
a statement she makes.

Seductive and alluring
for romance,
all part of the performance.
Power dressing for the boardroom
as promotion looms.

Whatever kind of woman she be
make no mistake,
a statement she makes.

Burning of the Bra

What is the meaning of this?
in its fireless state,
a bodice, a vest,
the creator of so much.

A pair of mobiles it encased
regardless of size or race.
Calico, cotton or lace
are often put through their pace

A restraint, a supporter
or a controller.
Femininity, feminism or
masculinity.
Wear it or burn it.

The size dictates the flame,
the wearer will never again be the same.
Liberator, dictator
or speculator.
To use or be used,
amused or abused.
Wear it or burn it.

In the Name of Love

At the alter they stood
as many thought they would or should.
          Their dying love for each other
they pledged
be it at the pub or in the bed.

The feast that followed
          was from money borrowed.
Eat today, worry tomorrow.
Like the sparrow they built
their nest,
          a place to play and be at rest.
Survival of their love
for each other
          time alone will be the test.

Some relatives laughed
and joked,
          others appeared half soaked.
At the couples expense
fun was poked.

Skeletons from the cupboards
on both sides came tumbling
out of mouths.
          Best man and master of ceremony
had to shout
"Have some respect you louts!"

Much dancing and laughter
was followed by disaster,
          it couldn't have happened any faster
as guests danced to the music
on the blaster.
          In a sudden flash the wedding cake crashed.
as it was bashed by a staggering man.

Too much ale was the tale.

The honeymoon
came and went so soon.
          This was in early June.

In July this is no word of lie.
reality sets in
          and things began to look grim.
The new bride no longer
looking slim.

A baby was born
The bride now a wife and mother,
her love was torn.
          Groom now a husband and father.
looking so forlorn.
So down to the pub he went
with no relent.
          His hard earned cash for this event,
in his mind it was cash well spent.

Ten years on
lots have gone on.
Weight gain and financial loss,
          two point five children in tow
and not much more to show.

Their love for each other
stood the test of time,
          in the pub and in the bed
as they both did pledge.

The Affair

I am the pollen,
you are the bee
come spread and bathe
yourself in me.

For my golden dust
you must lust.
To you and only you
my heart I entrust.

Buzz around me
as you please.
Love me from head to knees.
Kiss me, squeeze me,
tease me,
appease me,
don't ever leave me!
The magic of your favour
is our enriched love
my honey.

No Ask Me Fe Choose

Jamaican cuisine is second to none,
it's fit for a King or a Queen.
The food is sweet,
the food is nice,
never bland but full of spice.

Try it once,
try it twice,
you hook for life!
Food heaven not food hell,
so exotic and hypnotic,
it can cause a spell.

My favourite dish,
ackee and saltfish.
Other delicacies
are there to please
like the bun and cheese,
the rice and de peas.

Me lub unoh,
but lub me food
so no badda ask me fe choose,
cause unoh might just loose.

Caribbean Life

What is in a name for a region of islands
Surrounded by sun, sea and sand?
Exotic fruit, birds and trees,
These are but a few to please.
The words to be heard are
Caribbean life.

C is for Culture

A is for all alluring and appealing

R is for reggae and razzmatazz

I is for indulgence

B is for bright and beautiful

B is for Bountiful
E is for enchantment and entertainment
A is for adorable
N is for nature's gift to mankind, oh so natural

L is for living

I is islands so idyllic

F is for food and festivity

E is for excitement and ecliptic

Caribbean life is not without struggle and strife
But also offers many things that are oh so nice.
To be precise it is a privilege
If you've been thrown
That dice.

Senorita Butterfly

Senorita butterfly,
you are nature in motion,
gracefully you glide and hover
over blooming plants and shrubs
in idyllic locations,
sitting briefly where ever takes your fancy.
Peaceful and tranquil is your habitat.

Senorita butterfly,
your beauty no one can deny.
Spectacular and unique
is your art work of markings and colours,
impossible for other Senoritas to follow.

Colour Me Red

From head to toe
I could be clothed in any colour I chose
But colour me ***red***
Is what I said.

Bold statements I make
So much could be at stake.
Being ***red*** means
I am bright and vibrant
Strong and bold
Whether it be hot or cold.
Fiery, burning with desire
To young and old I am told.
Colour me ***red***
Is what I said.

I symbolise many things
Good or bad I am in the bag
Here are but a few
I chose to share with you.
At the bank
Regardless of rank
I could be in the ***red***
Long before the will is read.
Colour me ***red***
Is what I said.

Wine in my colour
Is palatable and rich
And is served with many a dish
Enhancing cuisine
fit for a king or a queen.
Colour me ***red***
Is what I said.

Some brides my colour
They cannot hide
As they wore me with great pride.
Power dressing is my business
My act of transformation
Is sheer elation.
From girl to womanhood
Ugly ducklings to beautiful swans
I transcend.
Colour me ***red***
Is what I said.

Socialist and communist
Is also on my list.
Left wing, right wing
Or centre of the party.
In the bed or under the bed.
Colour me ***red***
Is what I said.

Diss Lickle Fool Fool Dry Foot Gal

Diss lickle fool fool dry foot gal,
pickney inna har han
yet she hab no man,
diss lickle fool fool dry foot gal.

What she need fe understand,
immaculate conception or one night stan,
she still have a pickney in har han,
diss lickle fool fool dry foot gal.

Ku pon har head,
ku pon har face,
a real disgrace.
Head no comb,
face no wash,
yet she still a splash the *cash,*
diss lickle fool fool dry foot gal.

What she need indeed,
if as a single mom she is to succeed,
is get har bursary,
put pickney a nusery,
education on the way,
preparing for that rainy day,
diss lickle fool fool dry foot gal.

Diss lickle dry foot gal,
immaculate conception or one night stand,
tek charge of har educational plan
for herself and har pickney in har han,
now she's a proud lickle educated dry foot gal.

No badda

Buoy nung yu lef school
a weh yu gwine do wid yu life?
No badda tink sey yu ago tap a yard
an play no video game
til yu brain tun lard!
yu betta tink bout yu future
an go learn computer.

Dem style weh yu deh pap
we ha fe tap
when yu get yu lap tap.

No badda fe tell me bout noh rap
an all dat clap trap.
Me a yu madda an
me know bess.
Noh mek me ha fe go
beat me chess.

Yu betta tek yu self dung a di career centre
dem will pint you inah de career direction,
or gwaan a di college
an go full up you head
wid a hole heap a knowledge!

***Big** Issue*

Uprooted and plucked from a land
rich in culture yet harsh and volatile,
a place that screams you can be seen
but you shall not be heard,
this is the unwritten word.
Unfilled holes where my roots used to be
like smouldering volcanic craters with ash,
trampled upon, like unattended, unidentified graves.

Barred from my own country,
where else will I gain entry?
Criterion must be filled,
answers and evidence to a barrage of questions
I must give.
Scattered not sown,
no home to call my own.
Any bed will do
for a refugee or an asylum seeker like me.

Transported under the cover of darkness
with damaged, withered roots.
Soon to be thrown or dumped
onto unknown soil like quicksand.
Asylum seeker or refugee?
What will my status be?
As my drooping leaves inhales the future
of a newly found land,
can they exhale the past
from where my deep roots once did stand?

Can the doors of my heart
which is heavy as steel girders
yet fragile like delicate glass
be safely closed from the past?
as I shift my focus from
surviving life
to living life.

Inhaling the strength and freedom
whilst exhaling restriction and fear.

The **Big Issue**,
scattered not sown,
will I have enough determination to live?
Can I gain enough strength to love?
Will there be enough energy to gain freedom
whilst in a permanent state of gruelling exile?
Will my damaged roots ever penetrate
the new soil to which I am now bound,
whilst craving for that familiar cultural ground?

A Stopping Place Called Refuge

Hurry hurry, Quickly! Quickly!
my father used to say
every second of the day.
We are being watched.
A plan must be hatched,
my family is so unsafe
on this our ancestral patch.

Bang! Bang! Bang!

Hurry hurry, Quickly! Quickly!
Get out of the bed
my mother said.
I could tell from the blank
glazed look in her eyes
that my father was already dead.
Dead! dead! dead!

Hurry hurry, Quickly! Quickly!
my mother said.
The immediate thought in my head
screamed revenge! Avenge!
My eyes blazing,
heart pounding,
I was trembling.
The myriad of emotions were suffocating,
even intoxicating.
The sound of my mother's voice
jolted me back to something,
reality or insanity.

Hurry hurry, Quickly! Quickly!
my mother said.
We need another place to stop,
a place of refuge.

I watched the tears streaming down my sister's face,
we are off to that place of grace.
My brothers snivelling,
their stifling whimpering cries
filled the air.

Hurry hurry, Quickly Quickly!
my mother said.
Like bats out of hell we ran
to our old battered van.
As my sister fell,
I realised this was our hell.
In the middle of the night
not a single soul in sight.
Surely this cannot be right.
I am a refugee in my own country
seeking sanctuary.

Hurry hurry, Quickly! Quickly!
Get out of the van!
my mother said.
Our only possession
a blanket each in hand
as in the church we stand.
Sanctuary but not freedom,
like a King without a Kingdom.

Hurry, hurry, Quickly! Quickly!
Our first stopping place called refuge,
I know for sure
it will not be the last
as time passed.
Across the border we must pass
to another stopping place called refuge
with those piercing words
ringing in my ears.
Hurry hurry, Quickly! Quickly!

Putting In Appearance

"Mother who is that man?"
the son asked.

"Boy it's you father!"

"You mean as in father, papa, daddy?"

"Boy what kind of foolishness you talking?"

"But mother if he is my father,
how comes he is like a stranger?
I thought he was the lone ranger,
the clothes arranger
and you are the laundrette operator.
I know he brings you one
and two cigarette
and tell you not to fret.

At times I believe him was the loan shark
because he mostly come after dark.
He bring his clothes to wash
and sometime him trousers
for you to patch.
When him leave you sey
you miss you watch.

Him come fe five minutes,
sit down in chair,
cock up him foot,
reading the paper
as if him have no care,
then him ask you if you
have money to spare.

Mother him collect the clothes them
you wash and iron
him put on clean one,
slam the door and gone!

Then in a month or two
him reappear,
somebody knock pon de door,
it's the taxi man asking for him fare."

"Hey son" *says the man to the boy*
"you must respect me because I am
your father!"

"Father!" *the boy replied*
"I have a name for you."

"What name?"

"You name Bio"

The mother said
"What you call you father?"

The boy said
"him name Mr BF, Biological Father.

He comes four to five times a year,
him never have anything to share.
Him here and him not here.
Here today gone tomorrow
causing you mother
a whole heap of bother.

Him come with top hat on him head,
umbrella in a him hand,
dark glasses pon him face.
Yes him have another name
Mr Poser.

I did see you mother putting a picture

of him on the fridge door.
Some kind of memory
of what him look like
you are trying to secure,
for what reason I am unsure.

Something else I don't understand,
so hey man" *said the boy,*
"please give me a helping hand.
When me first notice you
come and cock up yu foot,
it was only me mother and me,
now there's six of we.
Here is not just a laundrette,
a restaurant or a money lender
but a baby making factory
for **you** Mr Biological father."

Mother Dear

Thank you mother
for giving birth to me.
A better mother you could never be.
On me perfect love, you bestowed,
unconditional love to you I owed,
from me to you
that is how it ought to be.

You wiped my tears
and stroked my hair
relieving all my fears
as you sat me down on your favourite chair.

When I fell from the tree
and hurt my knee,
your love for me was plain to see.
You was hurting as much as me,
gently cleaning my wounds.
You would go hungry so that I could eat,
I had so many special treats.

Now that you are older
and cannot see or hear very clear,
your eyes and ears I am proud to be,
mother dear you are so precious to me.

So Over U Partner

The first time I had you, you were all over me,
on my lips and down my chest
I had to stop and have a rest.

My eyes were barely at my knees
and I was being taught to say please,
I remember clearly you were very tasty hot & delicious.

As time passed,
I gasped
you were so intense,
I had to have you from January to December
come rain or shine
you were mine,
hot or cold
you were my partner to have and hold.

My mother claims you was good for me,
I had no choice I had to have you,
even when I was sick, always on a Saturday
never on a Sunday.
Sometimes you were thin
other times you were thick,
at times you were plain, red or brown,
light or heavy.

You was always wet, hot and bubbly,
all over the house I could smell you,
you became my tormentor.
Over and over again once every week you would strike,
when I had you I would sweat
until I was wet.

Every time I heard your name
it drove me insane.
Admittedly there were times when I longed for you,

my mother could not get enough of you,
to her you was the perfect medicine
to me you was menacing.
I craved and prayed for the day when I did not have to see you
or have you again.

Sweet seventeen came
and put an end to that game.

Yes! Yes! Yes!

So

Over

U

PARTNER

Have you guessed?
Yes it is the traditional West Indian
Saturday soup!

Tears So Sweet

Oh my love you are my precious dove.
My treasure trove,
you are the one I chose.
My heart and yours beating as one
as strands of our love entwined
you blew my mind.

I cannot separate myself from you
and will always remain true.
My love for you will stay as fresh as
the morning dew
sparkling like all things new.

As you are my honey,
I pray that I am your comb,
you are the Queen bee sitting on my throne.
You will never be alone.

Deeper than the ocean is my love for you.
It cannot be measured with gold or silver.
Whenever I think of you, my heart goes a quiver.
I scarcely can go to sleep.
At times I even weep.
Oh tears so sweet.

At the sound of your name
my excitement I cannot contain.
To this I feel no shame.
My angel, my shining star,
my heart will always be wherever you are,
near or far.
My dove,
My love.

Women

Women you are the salt of the earth,
this is your given status from birth.
Women of all races
with beautiful faces,
some sitting in high places.

Daily multitasking is your business.
Going to work,
cooking, cleaning
washing, ironing,
feeding the baby.
Sometimes you are even called a lady
not forgetting a bitch & a cow
when you refuse to bow.

You are the nations' wealth
promoting strength and health
without any uncertainty
you are a precious commodity.
Daughter, wife, sister,
aunty, mother or grandmother,
you are the brightest of scholars
and the greatest teachers.
As the saying goes,
behind every successful man
is a strong woman.

What is the meaning of the word women?

W = wonderful
O = Organiser
M = Mother & motivator
E = Educator
N = Negotiator

Women you are the salt of the earth,
this is your given status from birth.
The glue that holds
everything and everyone together.
You know you are the best but for
men's sake give it a rest!

Hands on Father

When my mother ran away
with my father I had to stay.
That's the chair where he used to sit
to polish the shoes,
to mend the clothes,
darn the socks
and knit the hats,
yes knit the hats!

He wiped my nose,
cleaned my toes,
washed my hair,
took me here, took me there.
Years of love he laboured
as his affection I savoured.
He was not phoney,
he was homely.

He was my sister, brother,
aunty, uncle,
mother and father
and if I could have chosen a parent
there would be no other.

He taught me so many things,
how to be gentle yet strong,
to know right from wrong.
His paternal influence
on me has impacted positively
on society that's the reality.
Male parenting can be everything.

I know I was his greatest treasure.
At times I knew he was lonely
as he could not indulge
in many pleasures.

I loved my father beyond words.
Now that he has passed away
and no longer here in the flesh,
Fathers' day without one so dear,
has left me in great despair,
knowing that for the one I held
in such high esteem
fate has decided the most extreme.

I am still weeping like fine rain
although my heart
is likened to a tropical storm,
my memories of my father
are all good,
no matter how much I reflect,
I had no wants nor neglect
just much respect.
A girl has no greater gift
to receive than the love and warmth
of a hands on father or
did I hear you say a modern man?
A great role model
to reflect on.

Sweet Sweet Love of Mine

Sweet Sweet love of mine
Everything about you I adore
Can a love be so pure?

You are as gentle as the morning breeze
Always aiming to please
At this moment in time
My heart you have completely seized.

Sweet Sweet love of mine
All other offers of love I will decline
As you will always be my valentine
Sweet Sweet love of mine.

Do you Remember?

Do you remember?
Long time ago,
how we all sat and ate together,
some of us would have to go
in an hour or so,
but due to friendship
we had to show.

Bread, tea and cakes
was our treat
every time we meet.

Do you remember?
How we talked
and laughed,
putting the world to right
was our delight.
Bitchiness sometimes got in the way
whilst we had our say.

Looking back now on
how we were dressed,
I must confess,
your hat, my frock
today we would be
a laughing stock,
a real culture shock.

Do you remember?
That day in September
when there was a rainfall,
I met Paul and forgot to call.
From grace I did fall
to Coventry I was sent
until I did relent
promising total commitment.

With resentment I complied,
I even lied.

Do you remember?
The day when there was only bread to be had.
The rugged table looked so drab
but we were glad
that a pound or two we would lose.

Do you remember?
when many said,
our friendships would not last.
Now time has past
we are still steadfast,
life has been a blast.
I rcmcmbcr.
Do you remember?

Mind

Isabella lay in the bed
The pillow squashed to her head
Her visitors was not sure
Whether she was alive or dead.

As she lay motionless
Wired up to the machinery
And other gadgetry
She hatched her plan
On how to net her man.
His name is Dan
For a living he drove a van.

The nurse came and interrupted
Her thoughts.
Isabella she said it is time for your scan.
The picture she could not understand
From the doctor she needed
A helping hand.

My dear he said
No need to stay in bed.
The scan shows there is nothing in your head

A tear or two fell
As she politely told him
To go to hell.

Passion

I love you, I love you.
Deep as the sea
is my love for thee.
You are the cream in my coffee
and the sugar in my tea.
When I found you,
my lover and my friend
I prayed our love
would never end.

You've turned my night into day,
I clearly remember
it was in the month of May.
With you forever I will stay.
Whenever I'm with you
the feeling of being so secure
lurked in my heart,
with love so pure.
There is nothing
I cannot endure.
I love you, I love you, I love you.

One plus one

The true equation of intimate love
is one plus one
since time began.

Sale!

The sign in the shop window reads
CLEARANCE
It is your last chance.

I looked hard and fast
at the goods displayed
and the intriguing ways in which
they were laid,
quickly I moved away
as I did not plan to stay.

I gave a second glance,
as if I was in a trance.
I made a stance
to brave this crowd.
I thought one needs to have endurance
and definitely some insurance.
Awakened from my state of daze
as I gazed,
I could not believe my eyes.
Could they be telling me lies?

I watched in horror
at this past time terror.
A woman in brown,
her face framed in a frown,
tugged and pulled and
tugged and pulled a red jumper
made from wool
away from the arms
of a girl who looked quite alarmed
yet remained calm.
As the girl let go the woman in brown
landed on her bum
taking with her a tidy sum
of anything and everything
that was in her path,
people, dresses, skirts and shirts.

Trousers and jumpers
were strewn to the floor.
I was now standing on the inner side
of the door
feeling quite unsure.
Should I continue in
or should I retreat?
The latter would spell defeat.
I did not move my feet
but was propelled by a fleet
of clearance shopaholics
This was no frolic!
Shunted straight to the section
displaying the sheets and
who did I meet?

The woman in brown
with her face framed in a frown,
she was heavily built
and was tugging and pulling
and tugging and pulling at a quilt
from a woman who was slightly built.
Quilted fibres filled the air,
many stand and stare,
the woman in brown did not care.

Walk away I must,
I cannot be dealing with
all this fuss.
To the stairs I took
giving the escalator a miss.
I will go to the first floor
to have a look
at shoes and books.

Guess what?
The woman in brown,
the escalator she did take
make no mistake.

She was pulling and tugging
at shoes and boots,
her hands now full with all the loot.

My visit to the theatre
can wait for much later,
I was already captive
to this theatrical caper.

Take my word,
if you like cabaret,
visit a clearance store
for sure.
It will be in disarray
take my tip,
you must be equipped
with endurance and
a very good insurance!

Christmas a Come

Christmas a come,
Christmas a come,
mek we go and
have some fun!

Shop shop
until you drop.
Plenty of gifts for you
to wrap,
Christmas a come,
Christmas a come.

Jingle bells
or juggle bills,
tills are ringing,
coffers are filling,
loan sharks are singing.
Christmas a come,
Christmas a come.

Chief execs from banks
to energies,
this is one of their strategies,
rob from Peter
to pay Paul.
We are Peter,
they are Paul.
Christmas a come,
Christmas a come.

Christmas come
and Christmas gone.
Pay day loans lingers on.
Soon and very very soon
Christmas a come,
Christmas a come.

Christmas Gone Pon Holiday

Christmas gone pon holiday,
hip hip hooray.
No trees to buy or decorate,
no cake for you to bake.
On line or in the shops,
they will not get
your hard earned cash.
No need for any
last minute dash.

Christmas has gone pon holiday
Hip hip hooray.

No pheasants
or presents to buy,
no extended family dinner
to organise,
then to endure all that noise.

No Grandad without his hair
sitting in his favourite chair,
party hat struggling
to stay on his head
makes Aunty Gracey see red
as his teeth fell from his mouth.
No Aunty Gracey to shout
"put your teeth back in
and stop breaking wind!"

Christmas gone pon holiday
Hip hip hooray.

Listening to tales of yester years,
enough to have you shedding tears.
All those skeletons in the cupboards
can stay for yet another year.

Christmas gone pon holiday
Hip hip hooray.

The Man on the Bus

On the back seat of the bus he sat face all gaunt,
eyes so sad, in his heart he wished
that he was still a lad.

Deepest blue eyes you ever did see
staring at the person sitting next to me.
He was lost in thought
as his attention was sought
by the inspector checking
for cheats in the seats.

His eyes looking blank,
my heart sank.
Ticket in his outstretched hand,
he shouted out loud
"I used to be in a band!"
His lips did not move
His face remained expressionless
as he uttered yet again,
"I am in a mess
but you all could not care less."
Heads of passengers a good few
turned and gazed to see who had lost a screw.

As the man got up and pressed the bell,
it appeared as though he had cast a spell.
Passengers froze in their seats
as they gazed.
He had a story to tell.

The journalist sitting on the back seat
of the bus observing and listening to all
that was said recognised that with this caper
his paper would sell.

Pen, paper and camera at the ready,
a scoop he thought.
The bus jolted to a halt.

The man continues to speak.
“I am not mad
I am not bad,
Yes I am sad.
I used to be jack the lad.”

The door of the bus opened.
The man stepped forward
then he looked back,
his blue eyes met
with mine
He smiled, I smiled back.
He said **“I wish I was black.”**
Everyone looked shocked.

He got off the bus.
The silence turned into a buzz.
The driver shook his head
some passengers muttered
he is mad.
Others said no he is sad.

As I reached my stop I got up
turned and looked around.
The buzzing had stopped.
There was not a sound.
I shouted “**Lord I am glad that I am black!”**

The Flickering Light

In the kitchen Mary stood
        gazing at the flickering light
in the ceiling.
        The pain she was feeling was flickering bad,
with hands on her behind
        a disco sprung to mind
as the flickering made her quite blind.
        "Flick me" she said.

In walked Reg,
        his hands full with fruit and veg.
"Flick that switch" he said
        "it's really doing my flicking head.

The fruits are for pickling."
        said Reg
Mary gazed at Reg,
        the fruit and veg
and then the flickering light
        above her head.
"Flick you" she said
        "I am going to my flicking bed."

The fruit and veg
        Reg laid neatly on the table's edge.
His eyes glazed over
        from the flickering light
above his head
        and all he could see was pure red.
"Flick that!"
        He said.
        "I'm off to the flicking potting shed!"

Mosaic

Tropical rainforest
At work or at rest,
Broken or unbroken,
Nature has spoken.

You are the most diverse of all habitats,
Trees, animals, insects and maybe bats.
Hundreds of different species of trees
And other vegetation contribute to your
Rich diversity
And identity
Varying in ages
And stages.

Trees die, they fall and lie.
Mosaic of gaps are formed,
Species changes,
Gaps rearranges
As your canopy regenerates
Creating such beautiful patterns
In different shapes and sizes.
The most awesome of colours;
Rust, brown, red and orange
Presents mosaic magnifica
Like a Phoenix rising
Your greens
Can be clearly seen in its vastness.

Browns and rusts illuminates
As your body rejuvenates,
Sheer radiance penetrates
From patches of light
Day and night.

Atmospheric sound is all around
Enhancing all in sight
The ever changing light.

A private habitat you probably would like to be
But with such beauty you are what many
Wants to see.

As humans trespass on your terrain
Your structure cannot remain the same
As seed and seedlings germinates from old
New mosaic gaps will unfold.
The survival of all forest species
Depends on how they adapt
To your ever changing habitat.

(Author's interpretation of the exhibit entitled 'The wax room' by Ken Parsons from the 2004 'Forest' exhibition at Wolverhampton Art Gallery.)

Window to the Soul

I looked into his eyes and was transfixed by what
I see or could not see.
The white area or sclera as it's called,
so dense even tense,
not giving anything away.
As he blinked the area appeared pink,
I continued to think.

My gaze fixed and focussed on
the centre of his eyes.
The darkest brown you ever did see,
all shiny and glazed,
he looked dazed.
The pupil of his eyes made contact
with mine,
they were ready to dine.

Fixation and enlargement,
I was transported and elevated
to another level.
His eyes was no longer a window
but an open door.

Inviting, enticing and exciting,
pupils entwined and searching
for the soul.
This is the right mould.
Soul mates we became,
a date was made
yet no words were spoken.
Our eyes was fixed to the prize.
A window to the soul.

Whutliss Harry

It was on independence day
dare I say, that whutliss Harry
tell me him sarry
but me hear it all before,
when all de sordid details
he did outpour.

Not one woman or two
but four.
To this day
I am still unsure.
Many times he needed the cure,
as by no means
these women were pure.

Such lewd behaviour
I could not ignore.
Number four even came
to knock on my door.
Kicks to her arse
and other parts I did pass,
Nobody nah tie me out
fe go eat no grass.
Independence day will not be
my cross!

Just Amazing

Oh wonderful, intriguing and cunning one,
your ever changing face has graced
mother earth
from the time of your birth,
this epitomised your girth.
North, East, West or South,
it's your shout.

Many titles you possess
but you could not care less
how you are addressed.
These are but a few,
so what is new?
Mangrove, swamp,
forest, jungle
and now bunker
your title stamp.

Many connotations is the interpretation
for your reputation,
implying protection and defence.
Danger lurking, unsolved mysteries,
magical happenings.
Your habitat dictates
numerous colours and a camouflage of
greens, browns, yellows, reds, oranges and blues.

Man-made works tries to imitate,
for what they are worth
Oxygen the liquid of life you generate,
its' absence would seal the human fate.
To this ecologist and botanist has agreed
and many others indeed.

You are Mother Nature at her best,
passing the scientific test.

Encapsulating lush vegetation.
As the sun interjects,
what is the effect?
Humid temperature,
vapour to mist,
who could resist?

Density and darkness
in your vastness.
Sunshine and rain
all adds to your fame.
Animals and birds
can be seen and heard.
Many artists have captured your beauty,
it is their ethical duty.

Snakes and spiders,
lions and tigers,
survival of the fittest not the weakest
is of significant interest,
nature at its' best,
inviting yet frightening.

Human emotions and your beauty are entwined
from the not so ridiculous
to the sublime.
Colours blazing and blending,
the magic is never ending.
Oh wonderful, intriguing and cunning one
you are just amazing!

(Author's interpretation of the exhibit entitled 'Bunker' by G Brecht from the 2004 'Forest' exhibition at Wolverhampton Art Gallery).

Independent Woman

As an independent woman,
me noh need noh whutliss man,
dem no fit inah fe me plan.

Sistas unoh undastan,
it wud be fe me bad luck
fe pick up one a dem ole buck,
who noh wangh fe wuk,
an unoh dun know sey dat suck.

Me noh wangh fe be no baby madda
fe go deal wid all dat kine ah badder
wid nedda twenty madda.

Me a wife materal,
dat mean me special.
As a wife me hab me right,
me noh hab no need fe fight
wid ebry ooman in sight,
me kan walk and hole me
head up high.

Me kan buy me own clothes
and me own hair, pay me own fair,
dribe me own car.
Disyah ooman cuming from far.
Me is a independent woman,
my name is resilliance,
so all unoh useless Ustaces out deh,
just kip unoh distance!

When Love Arrives

True love can take some time to arrive.
It can slowly creep
into your space
or sometimes
it's been there all
along
right in your face.

When love arrives
strive to keep it alive,
suffocate it and it will die.
Love must be nurtured
or it will walk out that door.

The Boss

I am the boss,
the buck stops with me.
I don't give a toss,
success is the key.

Responsibility without authority sucks,
I get the blame
but not the fame,
what is there to discuss?

I cannot hire,
I cannot fire,
I cannot climb any higher,
the situation is dire.

Knowledge is power
and power is knowledge.
I have the knowledge
yet I have no power.

I am a small fish in a large pond
that is filled with complexities.
A pond which looks grand
but not conducive to my abilities.
I am a cog in a wheel
that I cannot control,
my thunder they've stole.

Responsibility without authority sucks.
I get the blame
but not the fame
what is there to discuss?

I have the ambition,
I have the drive,
I have the conviction
yet I fail to strive.
I had my goal in sight,
flight from the big pond I took,

my own business was right
as in the future I looked.
I am now a big fish in a small pond.

I have the responsibility,
I have the knowledge,
I have the authority,
I have the power.
Power is knowledge,
knowledge is power,
now I can hire,
now I can fire.
I have climbed so much higher.
I am the boss!

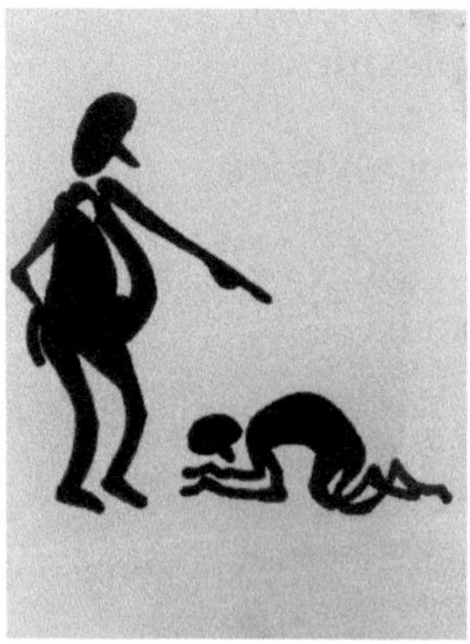

Freedom

In my dreams I fly away,
effortless and feeling free like a bird.
In my dreams I had huge wings,
like an aeroplane I darted high
above the clouds using my feet
like powerful propellers.
Breath taking scenery,
all around encapsulating
many a magnificent sight and sound.
Riotous is my subconscious
as I constantly drifted in and out
of a conscious state.
Reoccurring are my dreams
or so it seems.

Purrrrrrrfect!

Big cat,
little cat,
fat cat,
we are all in it together.

Oh no we are not!
I have no moat,
I have no boat,
I barely can keep afloat.
You greedy contented cat!

ME-OW?
Don't be so catty about
me being a millionaire.
Keep your little paws out of my
big fat affair.
Big cat, little cat, fat cat.

We can't all be................. ***purrrrrrrfect!***

What If?

What if we could love everyone?
woman child or man,
it would be grand
in this blessed land.

What if the world was square?
Would we all stand still and stare?
And not on the move like a merry go round
now that the world is round.

What if everyone had black, brown, white and yellow spots?
Instead of any single colour.
No dominance, no subordinates just equality.

What if there was no change in seasons?
and it was only summer, autumn, winter or spring.
Would we still hear the birds sing?
Would the earth yield its crops?
Would the trees be green, yellow or brown?
with branches swaying in the wind.

What if there was no sea or ocean?
Would there be knowledge of other nations?
And where would the fishes be?
What if we were all rich, who would do the chores?
Who would be serving instead of being served?

What if there were no nights, only days?
Would the moon and its' stars be gone?
And the sun alone brightly shone,
rising and setting or forever beaming.

What if I could not think or even blink?
This page would be blank with no trace of ink.

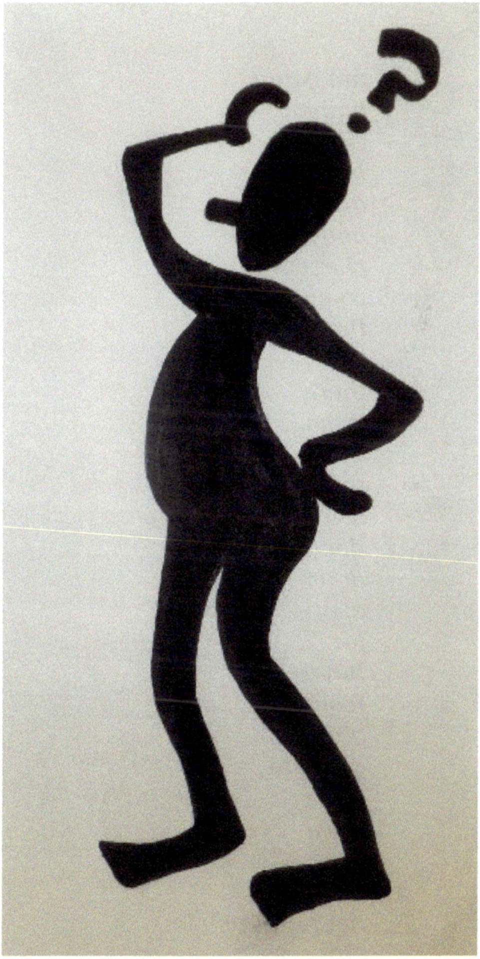

Glossary

Patois	**English**
ago	*am going*
badda	*bother*
bess	best
betta	*better*
bout	*about*
buoy	*boy*
chess	*chest*
cuming	*coming*
dat	*that*
de	*the*
deh	*there*
dem	*them*
diss	*this*
disyah	*this here*
dribe	*drive*
dun	*done*
dung	*down*
ebry	*every*
fe	*for*
fi	*for/to*
fool fool	*foolish*
gal	*girl*
gwine	*going to*
ha	*have*
hab	*have*
har	*her*
hey	*hi*
hole	*hold and whole*
kan	*can*
kine	*kind*
kip	*keep*
ku pon	*look upon*

lap tap	*laptop*
lef	*left or leave*
lickle	*little*
lub	*love*
madda	*mother*
mek	*make*
mumbo jumbo	*speaking rubbish*
nah tie	*not tying*
nedda	*another*
noh	*don't or any*
noh	*no*
nung	*now*
ole	*old*
ooman	*woman*
oonoo	*you all (more than one person)*
pap	*pop*
pickney	*child*
pint	*point*
pon	*on*
pon	*on*
sarry	*sorry*
sey	*say*
sistas	*sisters*
stan	*stand*
tap	*stop*
tek	*take*
tink	*think*
tun	turn
undastan	*understand*
unuoh	*all of you*
unuoh	*all of you*
wangh	*want*
weh	*what*
whutliiss	*worthless*
wid	*with*
wuk	*work*
yu	*you*

Glossary Phrases

Cock up him foot.

Put his feet up comfortably.

Dem no fit inah fe me plan.

They do not fit in my plan.

me noh need noh whutliss man!

I do not need any worthless man

Sistas unuoh undastan.

Sisters you all understand.

* 9 7 8 1 7 8 4 5 6 1 0 0 0 *

ND - #0097 - 060826 - C0 - 210/148/5 - PB - 9781784561000 - Gloss Lamination